No Grid survival projects

Unleash Your Inner Survivor, Learn
Essential Skills for Off-Grid Living
| A Comprehensive Guide to
Self-Reliance and Survival Mastery

Lemeul Thomas

1

Table of Contents

Introduction

In a world defined by connectivity and convenience, the notion of self-reliance often feels like a distant relic, an ancient art lost amidst the hum of modernity. Yet, as our dependency on external systems grows, the call for self-sufficiency becomes not just a skill but a necessity—an empowering choice to navigate life's uncertainties with resilience and mastery.

Welcome to "No Grid Survival Projects: Unleash Your Inner Survivor." This comprehensive guide isn't just a book—it's a beacon, a roadmap for those seeking to reclaim the art of self-reliance and embark on a transformative journey toward off-grid living and survival mastery.

Why does it matter? The relevance of this topic transcends trends; it speaks to the very core of our existence. In an era where disruptions to traditional systems are increasingly common, the ability to thrive independently becomes paramount. The art of off-grid living isn't merely a survival tactic; it's a lifestyle that fosters a profound connection with nature and empowers individuals to navigate life's challenges with confidence.

As an expert in nonfiction writing and a guide in navigating personal growth, I've witnessed the transformative power of embracing self-reliance. This book isn't just a compilation of techniques; it's a testament to the profound impact of self-sufficiency on our lives—a narrative woven with expertise, empathy, and a deep understanding of human resilience. This book serves as your trusted companion, guiding you through a rich tapestry of essential survival skills, fostering a mindset shift toward self-reliance, and nurturing a community committed to off-grid mastery.

Within these pages lies a treasure trove of knowledge—a journey divided into distinct yet interconnected chapters. We'll embark on an exploration of shelter building techniques, fire-starting methods, water sourcing and purification, foraging and wild plant identification, hunting, fishing, and trapping strategies, food preservation, off-grid cooking, community building, and much more.

Each chapter is not just a lesson—it's a doorway to a vital survival skill or a facet of off-grid living. But here's the teaser: there's more than meets the eye. Beyond mere instructions, this book unravels the emotional, mental, and communal aspects of self-reliance—showcasing not just how to survive, but how to thrive in harmony with nature.

And also You might wonder, "Is off-grid living feasible for me?" Fear not, dear reader. In addressing common concerns and objections, this guide dismantles apprehensions. Whether you're a novice or seasoned adventurer, this book meets you where you are, offering a pathway paved with practicality, empathy, and a supportive hand.

So, if you've ever felt the stirring call to be more than a passive recipient of convenience, if the allure of self-reliance beckons you to explore uncharted territories within yourself—this book is your invitation to embark on a transformative odyssey. Embrace it, engage with it, and let your inner survivor emerge.

Chapter 1:Embracing the Off-Grid Lifestyle

Living off the grid is not merely a physical departure from mainstream society; it's a profound shift in mindset and lifestyle. This chapter serves as a gateway into the world of off-grid living, exploring the fundamental principles of embracing self-reliance, understanding the off-grid mentality, and critically assessing the need for such a transformative way of life.

Embracing Self-Reliance

The Essence of Self-Reliance
At the heart of the off-grid lifestyle lies the essence of self-reliance – the ability to meet one's needs without undue dependence on external systems. Embracing self-reliance is not a rejection of community or cooperation but a recognition that true freedom stems from the ability to take control of one's destiny. It involves cultivating a mindset that values personal responsibility, resourcefulness, and the satisfaction derived from one's own efforts.

This section prompts readers to question the status quo and ponder the extent to which they rely on external sources for their daily needs. It challenges conventional thinking and encourages individuals to envision a life where they actively contribute to their well-being, reducing their environmental footprint and gaining a sense of empowerment in the process.

The Call of the Wild

Off-grid living is, in many ways, a return to a more primal state of existence. It beckons individuals to reconnect with nature, tapping into the ancient wisdom that sustained humanity for millennia. Embracing self-reliance involves learning from the natural world, understanding the ebb and flow of ecosystems, and adapting to the changing seasons.

Readers are guided through the process of embracing the wild as a source of inspiration and sustenance. Whether it's learning to identify edible plants, honing survival skills, or understanding the language of the land, this chapter emphasizes the transformative power of connecting with the natural environment.

Simplicity as a Virtue

In a world inundated with material excess, embracing the off-grid lifestyle often involves a shift toward simplicity. This section explores the virtue of living with less, focusing on the essentials, and finding fulfillment in the absence of unnecessary luxuries. Readers are encouraged to reassess their priorities, distinguishing between wants and needs, and discovering the liberation that comes with a minimalist approach to life.

Practical tips for decluttering, downsizing, and adopting sustainable consumption habits are woven into the narrative. Embracing self-reliance becomes not only a philosophy but a tangible, day-to-day practice that fosters a deeper connection with one's surroundings and a greater appreciation for the simple joys of life.

Understanding the Off-Grid Mentality

Resourcefulness Over Convenience

The off-grid mentality places a premium on resourcefulness, valuing the ability to adapt and innovate over the convenience of modern amenities. This section explores the shift from a consumer mindset to a creator mindset, where individuals actively participate in meeting their needs rather than relying on mass-produced solutions.

Readers are introduced to the idea that challenges are opportunities for growth and creativity. The off-grid mentality encourages the development of a diverse skill set, from carpentry to foraging, allowing individuals to navigate the complexities of life with a hands-on and proactive approach.

Thriving in Adversity

Off-grid living isn't without its challenges, and the off-grid mentality equips individuals with the resilience to thrive in adversity. This section delves into the psychology of facing uncertainties, overcoming setbacks, and learning from failures. Through real-life anecdotes and psychological insights, readers gain a deeper understanding of the mental fortitude required to weather the storms of off-grid living.

The off-grid mentality transforms obstacles into stepping stones, fostering a mindset that views setbacks as opportunities for learning and growth. By understanding and internalizing this mentality, individuals are better prepared to face the unpredictable nature of an off-grid lifestyle.

Environmental Stewardship

An integral aspect of the off-grid mentality is a profound sense of environmental stewardship. This section explores the responsibility that comes with living close to nature. Readers are encouraged to see themselves not as separate from the environment but as custodians of the land they inhabit.

Understanding the interconnectedness of ecosystems, the impact of human actions on the environment, and the importance of sustainable practices becomes paramount. The off-grid mentality fosters a deep respect for nature, inspiring individuals to tread lightly, minimize their ecological footprint, and actively contribute to the preservation of the planet.

Assessing the Need for Off-Grid Living

Personal Motivations

The decision to embrace an off-grid lifestyle is deeply personal, and this section guides readers through a process of self-reflection. By identifying and understanding their motivations, individuals can clarify whether off-grid living aligns with their values and aspirations.

Whether driven by a desire for greater autonomy, disillusionment with mainstream society, or a longing for a closer connection to nature, readers are prompted to explore the root causes behind their interest in off-grid living. This self-awareness forms the foundation for a sustainable and fulfilling off-grid experience.

Skills and Readiness

Off-grid living demands a set of practical skills and a readiness to face the challenges that arise. This section provides a comprehensive overview of the skills required, from basic survival techniques to sustainable living practices. Readers are encouraged to assess their current skill set and identify areas for improvement.

Practical exercises and resources are integrated to assist individuals in developing the necessary skills for off-grid living. Whether it's learning to grow food, purify water, or build a shelter, this chapter empowers readers to take tangible steps toward self-sufficiency.

Financial and Logistical Considerations

Beyond skills, financial and logistical considerations play a crucial role in the decision to go off-grid. This section prompts readers to assess their financial stability, explore alternative income streams, and plan for the initial transition to an off-grid lifestyle.

Practical advice on budgeting, income generation, and off-grid infrastructure is provided to help individuals make informed decisions. Understanding the financial and logistical aspects ensures a smoother transition and enhances the long-term viability of off-grid living.

In conclusion, Chapter 1 lays the groundwork for a transformative journey into off-grid living. Embracing self-reliance, understanding the off-grid mentality, and assessing the need for such a lifestyle form the pillars of a mindset that transcends the physical act of living off the grid. As readers delve into subsequent chapters, they carry with them a profound understanding of the principles that will shape their off-grid experience – a journey marked by self-discovery, resilience, and a harmonious relationship with the natural world.

Chapter 2:Essential Mindset and Preparation

Preparing for an off-grid lifestyle extends beyond mastering practical skills; it involves cultivating a resilient mindset, assessing risks, and mentally preparing for the unique challenges of living off the grid. This chapter delves into the psychological aspects of off-grid living, guiding individuals on how to develop a survivor's mindset, effectively assess risks, and prepare themselves mentally for the transition.

Cultivating a Survivor's Mindset

Resilience in Adversity

At the core of the off-grid experience lies the necessity for a survivor's mindset – an attitude that thrives in the face of challenges. This section emphasizes the importance of resilience, adaptability, and mental fortitude in navigating the uncertainties of an off-grid lifestyle.

Readers are encouraged to embrace challenges as opportunities for growth rather than insurmountable obstacles. Practical exercises and anecdotes from seasoned off-gridders help individuals understand how to cultivate resilience, bounce back from setbacks, and develop the mental stamina required for the unpredictable nature of off-grid living.

Self-Awareness and Adaptability

Understanding one's strengths, weaknesses, and limitations is crucial for thriving off the grid. This section guides readers through introspective exercises designed to enhance self-awareness. By acknowledging personal strengths and areas for growth, individuals can tailor their off-grid journey to align with their capabilities.

Adaptability, the ability to pivot and adjust to changing circumstances, is also explored. Readers learn to embrace uncertainty, develop creative problem-solving skills, and approach challenges with a flexible mindset. Cultivating adaptability ensures a smoother transition into an off-grid lifestyle and empowers individuals to thrive in diverse environments.

The Power of Positive Thinking

Optimism and a positive mindset are invaluable assets in the off-grid journey. This section explores the psychological benefits of maintaining a positive outlook amidst adversity. Readers discover techniques to reframe challenges, focus on solutions rather than problems, and cultivate an optimistic attitude that fuels resilience.

Through the exploration of positive psychology principles, individuals learn how to foster a mindset that not only endures but thrives in the face of hardship. The power of positive thinking becomes a cornerstone of mental preparation for off-grid living.

Assessing Risk and Planning Ahead

Identifying Potential Risks

Off-grid living introduces a unique set of risks that individuals must be prepared to navigate. This section prompts readers to conduct a comprehensive assessment of potential risks, ranging from natural disasters to economic instability. By identifying potential threats, individuals can better prepare and mitigate their impact.

Practical tools and guidelines aid in recognizing and categorizing various risks, allowing readers to prioritize and address them systematically. Understanding the specific challenges associated with off-grid living enables individuals to proactively plan and prepare for contingencies.

Strategic Planning and Contingency Measures

Planning ahead is essential for success in an off-grid lifestyle. This section focuses on the importance of strategic planning and the development of contingency measures. Readers are guided through the process of creating detailed off-grid plans that encompass emergency preparedness, resource allocation, and long-term sustainability.

Strategies for building resilient off-grid systems, such as alternative energy sources, food storage, and communication plans, are explored. Practical tips and case studies provide insights into effective planning techniques that enhance preparedness for a range of potential scenarios.

Financial Resilience and Sustainability

Financial stability is a critical aspect of off-grid living. This section addresses the importance of financial resilience and sustainable practices. Readers learn to assess their financial situation, explore income-generating opportunities, and develop strategies for financial self-sufficiency.

Budgeting tips, advice on reducing expenses, and generating income streams in remote settings are integrated into the narrative. Understanding the financial implications of off-grid living empowers individuals to make informed decisions and build a sustainable economic foundation.

Psychological Preparation for Off-Grid Living

Coping with Isolation and Loneliness Off-grid living, especially in remote locations, can lead to feelings of isolation. This section explores the psychological impact of solitude and offers strategies for coping with loneliness. Readers learn the importance of establishing connections, maintaining communication, and fostering a sense of community, even in remote settings. Practical advice on building social networks, engaging in hobbies, and nurturing meaningful relationships is provided. Psychological preparation involves recognizing the potential challenges of isolation and proactively addressing them to maintain mental well-being.

Embracing Solitude and Self-Reflection

Contrary to the challenges of isolation, solitude can also be a source of profound growth and self-discovery. This section encourages individuals to embrace solitude as an opportunity for self-reflection, introspection, and personal growth.

Readers explore techniques for mindfulness, meditation, and self-care that promote mental clarity and emotional resilience. Embracing solitude becomes a transformative experience, allowing individuals to deepen their understanding of themselves and their connection to the natural world.

Building Mental Resilience

The mental resilience required for off-grid living encompasses a spectrum of challenges. This section delves into stress management, emotional regulation, and strategies for maintaining mental well-being. Readers learn practical techniques to build mental resilience, including mindfulness practices, relaxation exercises, and stress-reducing activities.

Understanding the psychological demands of off-grid living enables individuals to develop coping mechanisms that enhance their ability to thrive in challenging environments. Mental preparation becomes an essential component of the holistic approach to off-grid lifestyle adaptation.

In conclusion, Chapter 2 serves as a comprehensive guide to the essential mindset and psychological preparation required for off-grid living. By cultivating a survivor's mindset, assessing risks, and psychologically preparing for the unique challenges of off-grid life, individuals embark on a journey that not only tests their practical skills but also nurtures their resilience, adaptability, and mental fortitude. The principles and practices outlined in this chapter lay a solid foundation for navigating the complexities of living off the grid with confidence and determination.

Chapter 3:Shelter Building Techniques

Shelter is the cornerstone of survival in any off-grid or wilderness setting. This chapter delves into the essential aspects of shelter building, covering the fundamentals, techniques for constructing temporary and permanent shelters, and the art of utilizing natural resources for construction purposes.

Understanding Shelter Basics

Shelter as a Fundamental Need
Shelter provides protection from the elements, maintains body temperature, and offers a sense of security. This section emphasizes the critical role of shelter in survival scenarios, highlighting its significance beyond mere physical comfort.

Readers grasp the importance of prioritizing shelter as one of the first tasks in any off-grid or wilderness situation.

Factors Influencing Shelter Design

Understanding the environmental factors that influence shelter design is crucial. Readers explore how terrain, climate, available materials, and personal needs impact the choice of shelter. From mountainous regions to dense forests or arid deserts, shelter requirements vary, and this section equips individuals to adapt their designs accordingly.

Shelter Components and Features

The anatomy of a shelter involves understanding its components: walls, roof, insulation, and flooring. Readers gain insights into the different types of shelters, from simple lean-tos to more complex structures like cabins or igloos. Moreover, the importance of features such as ventilation, waterproofing, and durability is elucidated to ensure a functional and safe shelter.

Building Temporary and Permanent Shelters

Temporary Shelter Techniques

In emergency situations or during initial phases of off-grid living, temporary shelters are essential. This section delves into various techniques for constructing temporary shelters using minimal resources. Methods such as debris huts, A-frame shelters, or tarp shelters are explored, providing step-by-step instructions and practical tips for quick and efficient construction.

Permanent Shelter Construction

For long-term off-grid living, durable and sustainable shelters are necessary. This part introduces readers to more advanced construction methods for permanent shelters. It covers traditional techniques like log cabin building, wattle and daub, or cob construction. Readers learn about the skills and tools required, as well as the considerations for choosing the right location and materials for lasting structures.

Structural Stability and Safety Measures

Ensuring structural stability and safety in shelter construction is paramount. This section emphasizes the importance of proper anchoring, load distribution, and adherence to safety standards. Readers gain an understanding of structural engineering principles, reinforcing their knowledge to build sturdy and safe shelters.

Utilizing Natural Resources for Shelter Construction

Foraging and Harvesting Building Materials

Nature provides a wealth of resources for shelter construction. This section educates readers on identifying and responsibly harvesting materials such as wood, bamboo, branches, leaves, or stones. Techniques for sustainably foraging building materials without causing harm to the environment are emphasized.

Crafting and Processing Natural Resources

Once materials are gathered, processing and crafting them for shelter construction is a skill in itself. Readers explore techniques for splitting wood, weaving branches, shaping stones, or using natural adhesives. Understanding these methods allows individuals to transform raw natural resources into functional building materials.

Sustainable Building Practices

The chapter concludes by advocating for sustainable building practices. Readers discover the importance of minimizing environmental impact by using locally sourced and renewable materials. Techniques like upcycling, repurposing, and adopting eco-friendly construction methods are highlighted, promoting a harmonious relationship between shelter construction and the environment.

Advanced Shelter Designs

Geodesic Domes and Earthbag Structures

Explore unconventional yet highly efficient shelter designs. Geodesic domes and earthbag structures offer unique benefits such as strength, energy efficiency, and adaptability to various terrains. Detailed instructions and considerations for constructing these innovative shelters are provided.

Treehouse Construction

Delve into the art of building elevated shelters using trees as the foundation. Learn about treehouse design principles, safety measures, and sustainable methods for integrating dwellings with natural surroundings while minimizing impact on the trees themselves.

Shelter Maintenance and Repair

Maintenance Practices for Longevity Understanding the importance of regular maintenance to ensure the durability of shelters. Learn about inspection routines, repairs for wear and tear, and seasonal maintenance tasks to preserve the integrity of temporary and permanent shelters.

Emergency Repairs and Improvisation Unforeseen circumstances can damage shelters. Discover quick-fix solutions and improvisation techniques using available resources for immediate repairs during emergencies. These skills are crucial for ensuring shelter functionality in unpredictable situations.

Shelter Customization and Personalization

Interior Design and Comfort

Explore ways to personalize and optimize shelter interiors for comfort and functionality. Tips on organizing space, incorporating furniture, and enhancing livability to create a cozy and efficient living environment.

Incorporating Sustainable Technologies

Learn about integrating off-grid technologies into shelters. Explore options for solar panels, rainwater harvesting systems, or passive heating and cooling techniques to make shelters more self-sufficient and eco-friendly.

Cultural and Historical Shelter Practices

Indigenous Shelter Building Techniques

Explore traditional shelter-building methods from diverse cultures around the world. Learn from the wisdom and techniques passed down through generations, understanding how different societies adapted their dwellings to their environments.

Historical Architecture and Modern Adaptations

Examine historical architectural styles and their relevance to modern shelter design. Discover how ancient building methods and aesthetics can be adapted and incorporated into contemporary off-grid living structures.

Community Building through Shelter Construction

Collaborative Shelter Projects

Explore the benefits of communal efforts in building shelters. Learn how collaborative projects within off-grid communities not only create durable structures but also foster a sense of community, cooperation, and shared responsibility.

Skill-Sharing and Workshops

Discuss the importance of skill-sharing sessions and workshops within off-grid communities. These opportunities not only teach shelter-building techniques but also create a sense of empowerment and self-sufficiency among community members.

In essence, Chapter 3 provides a comprehensive guide to shelter building techniques. From understanding the basics and designing shelters according to environmental factors to constructing temporary and permanent structures using natural resources, readers acquire the knowledge and skills necessary to create functional, safe, and sustainable shelters in off-grid or wilderness settings.

Chapter 4: Water Sourcing and Purification

Identifying Water Sources in the Wilderness

Understanding Water Sources
Exploring the diverse sources of water available in the wilderness is crucial. Readers learn to identify natural sources such as rivers, lakes, streams, and springs. Understanding the characteristics and reliability of each source is essential for ensuring a consistent water supply.

Collecting Water from Unconventional Sources
In some scenarios, finding potable water might require innovative approaches. This section covers unconventional sources like dew collection, transpiration bags, and digging for groundwater. These

methods offer alternatives when traditional water sources are scarce or contaminated.

Hazards and Contamination Risks

Understanding potential contaminants and hazards in natural water sources is paramount. Readers learn to identify signs of contamination, such as discoloration, odor, or visible particles. This knowledge is vital for selecting the most appropriate purification methods to render water safe for consumption.

Purification Methods and Techniques

Boiling and Pasteurization

One of the most efficient ways to cleanse water is to boil it. This section details the proper technique for boiling water to eliminate pathogens and contaminants. Additionally, the concept of pasteurization as an alternative method for water purification is explained.

Filtration and Straining Techniques

Explore various filtration methods using improvised filters made from natural materials like sand, gravel, and cloth. Readers learn about creating DIY filtration systems and straining techniques to remove sediment, debris, and larger particles from water.

Chemical Treatment and Disinfection

Understanding chemical treatments such as chlorine or iodine tablets is crucial. Detailed instructions on dosage, waiting periods, and the effectiveness of these chemical agents in disinfecting water are provided. Moreover, alternative natural disinfection methods are also explored.

Rainwater Harvesting and Conservation

Collecting Rainwater for Potable Use

Rainwater harvesting serves as an invaluable resource in off-grid or remote settings. Readers discover techniques for collecting and storing rainwater using simple systems such as rain barrels, gutters, and tarp catchments. The importance of filtration and treatment of collected rainwater is emphasized.

Sustainable Water Conservation Practices

Conserving water is vital in off-grid living to ensure a steady supply. This section explores practices like greywater recycling, water-saving strategies, and responsible usage habits. Readers gain insights into minimizing water waste and maximizing efficiency in water consumption.

Building Natural Water Storage Solutions

Learn about natural water storage solutions like ponds, cisterns, or dug wells. Understanding the construction

historical significance fosters an appreciation for its role in contemporary survival scenarios.

Psychological Comfort and Security

Beyond its practical uses, fire holds psychological value. It offers comfort, security, and a sense of companionship, especially in isolated or challenging environments. The emotional impact of fire on mental well-being during survival situations is discussed, highlighting its dual role as a physical and psychological survival tool.

Mastering Various Fire Starting Techniques

Traditional Methods: Flint and Steel, Bow Drill, and Hand Drill

Explore traditional fire-starting techniques passed down through generations. Detailed explanations and step-by-step guides illustrate the use of flint and steel, the bow drill method, and the hand drill technique. Readers learn the intricacies of these methods, including materials, technique precision, and troubleshooting common challenges.

Modern Tools: Lighters, Ferrocerium Rods, and Fire Pistons

Incorporating modern tools into fire starting methods is also crucial. Readers discover the advantages of using lighters, ferrocerium rods, and fire pistons. Understanding these tools' capabilities and limitations ensures a diversified skill set for starting fires in varying conditions.

Maintaining Fire in Challenging Conditions

Fire in Wet or Windy Environments

Challenges often arise when trying to maintain fire in adverse weather conditions. Learn specialized techniques for starting and preserving fire during rainy, windy, or snowy situations. Methods such as the upside-down fire, windbreak construction, or using natural windbreaks are detailed to maintain flames despite challenging weather.

Fire in High Altitudes or Cold Climates
Survival scenarios in high altitudes or cold climates present unique challenges for maintaining fire. Explore strategies for preserving heat, fuel conservation, and leveraging natural landscape features for shelter and insulation. Techniques like the Dakota fire hole or using rocks to reflect heat aid in overcoming these specific challenges.

Sustaining Fire for Long-Term Use
Understanding how to sustain fire for prolonged periods is vital for survival. Readers learn about fire management, fuel selection, and efficient fire-tending practices. Building and maintaining sustainable fire structures that burn steadily over extended

periods ensures a consistent source of warmth, light, and cooking heat.

Conclusion: The Significance of Fire Mastery

In conclusion, Chapter 5 highlights the pivotal role of fire as a survival tool. From its historical significance to the mastery of various fire-starting techniques and the challenges of sustaining fire in adverse conditions, readers gain comprehensive insights into harnessing fire for survival. Mastery of these techniques not only ensures the ability to start fires in diverse scenarios but also fosters a deeper appreciation for the elemental force that has shaped human existence.

Chapter 6: Foraging and Wild Plant Identification

This delves into the critical skill of foraging and wild plant identification, encompassing the identification of edible plants and berries, precautions against poisonous flora, and sustainable foraging practices essential for off-grid living or wilderness survival.

Identifying Edible Plants and Berries

Botanical Identification Basics
Understanding the basics of plant identification forms the foundation. Readers learn about leaf shapes, arrangements, and distinctive features that aid in identifying various plant species. Visual aids and descriptive guidance facilitate accurate plant recognition.

Edible Plant Families and Species

Explore common edible plant families and their species found in diverse environments. Detailed descriptions, images, and habitat information aid in identifying edible plants such as wild greens, roots, tubers, fruits, and berries. Emphasis is placed on easily recognizable and palatable species suitable for consumption.

Foraging Seasons and Locations

Understanding when and where to forage is crucial. Readers learn about seasonal variations in plant growth and the optimal times for harvesting specific wild edibles. Additionally, insights into various habitats like forests, meadows, or wetlands aid in locating abundant sources of edible plants.

Avoiding Poisonous Flora

Recognizing Toxic Plants

Identifying and avoiding poisonous flora is paramount. Detailed guidance is provided on recognizing common poisonous plants and their distinctive characteristics. This section emphasizes caution and thorough knowledge before consuming any wild plant.

Testing and Verification Methods

Readers discover methods for safely testing edibility, such as the universal edibility test and the skin test. These methods enable individuals to verify the safety of unknown plants before consumption, minimizing the risk of ingesting toxic species.

Sustainable Foraging Practices

Ethical Harvesting Techniques

Sustainable foraging emphasizes responsible harvesting practices. Readers learn about ethical approaches to foraging, including techniques for selective harvesting, leaving no trace, and respecting plant populations. By minimizing impact, individuals ensure the continued availability of edible plants in their natural habitats.

Plant Propagation and Cultivation

Encouraging the cultivation and propagation of edible wild plants promotes sustainability. Readers gain insights into methods for responsibly harvesting seeds, propagating edible species, and cultivating them in controlled environments, allowing for a sustainable and renewable food source.

Conservation and Preservation Efforts

Understanding the importance of conserving wild plant populations is crucial. Readers explore conservation efforts, including protecting natural habitats, supporting local biodiversity, and advocating for sustainable foraging practices to ensure the longevity of edible plant species.

Nutritional Value and Culinary Uses

Nutritional Benefits of Wild Edibles
Explore the nutritional profiles of various wild plants and berries. Detailed breakdowns of vitamins, minerals, and macronutrients present in these plants provide insights into their dietary value.

Culinary Applications and Recipes
Delve into the culinary versatility of wild edibles. Readers discover recipes and cooking techniques that showcase the flavors and textures of foraged plants and berries, encouraging experimentation in wild-inspired cuisine.

Medicinal and Herbal Applications

Medicinal Properties of Wild Plants
Discover the medicinal properties and traditional uses of wild plants. Insights

into herbal remedies, natural treatments, and holistic health benefits derived from these plants enhance their value beyond culinary purposes.

Herbal Crafting and Natural Remedies

Learn about crafting herbal remedies from foraged plants. From teas and tinctures to salves and poultices, readers explore methods for creating natural, plant-based remedies for various ailments.

Environmental Impact and Conservation

Foraging Ethics and Environmental Impact

Further exploration into ethical considerations in foraging practices. Discussions on the impact of foraging on ecosystems, biodiversity, and conservation efforts help readers make informed decisions.

Restoration and Regenerative Foraging

Understanding regenerative foraging techniques and their role in restoring ecosystems. Insights into practices that promote plant regeneration and habitat restoration contribute to sustainable foraging practices.

Advanced Plant Identification Skills

Plant Family Recognition
Going beyond basic identification to understand plant families and their characteristics. Readers delve into advanced identification skills to recognize plant relationships and broader botanical classifications.

Navigating Seasonal Variations and Adaptation

Understanding how seasonal changes and environmental adaptations affect plant characteristics. Insights into identifying plants across different seasons and varied environmental conditions enhance identification skills.

Expanding on these subsections provides a comprehensive understanding of foraging, from nutritional and medicinal aspects to environmental impact and advanced identification skills, offering readers a holistic view of incorporating wild plants into their lives responsibly and sustainably.

Harmonious Foraging for Sustainability

Chapter 6 underscores the significance of foraging and wild plant identification in off-grid living or wilderness survival. By mastering the identification of edible plants, avoiding poisonous flora, and adopting sustainable foraging practices, individuals not only acquire a valuable skill for acquiring food but also contribute to environmental conservation. Balancing the knowledge of wild edibles with responsible foraging practices fosters a harmonious relationship with nature while ensuring the availability of these resources for future generations.

Chapter 7: Hunting, Fishing, and Trapping

This explores the crucial skills of hunting, fishing, and trapping, encompassing techniques for survival, strategies for fishing in diverse environments, and effective methods for trapping to sustain oneself in off-grid living or wilderness survival scenarios.

Hunting Techniques for Survival

Understanding Prey Behavior and Habitats

Explore the behaviors and habitats of different game species. Readers learn about tracking, interpreting signs, and understanding animal behavior to locate and approach small animals effectively.

Firearms, Archery, and Primitive Hunting Tools
Delve into the use of firearms, bows, and primitive hunting tools for securing food. Detailed guidance on weapon selection, marksmanship, and primitive hunting techniques enhances hunting proficiency.

Stealth and Camouflage

Mastering stealth and camouflage techniques aids in approaching prey undetected. Readers learn about concealment, movement, and scent control to increase hunting success rates.

Advanced Tracking and Stalking

Delve deeper into advanced tracking methods, including interpreting animal prints, analyzing scat, and understanding territorial behaviors. Advanced stalking techniques enhance the ability to approach prey without detection.

Adapting to Various Terrains and Climates

Explore hunting strategies tailored to different terrains, from dense forests to open plains or mountainous regions. Understanding how to adapt hunting techniques to diverse climates and landscapes improves success rates.

Hunting Safety and Field Dressing

Discuss safety protocols during hunting expeditions, including firearm safety, wilderness first aid, and ethical handling of firearms. Additionally, insights into field dressing and processing game animals ensure safe and efficient utilization of harvested meat.

Fishing Strategies in Various Environments

Freshwater and Saltwater Fishing Techniques

Explore diverse fishing methods for freshwater lakes, rivers, and saltwater environments. Detailed instructions on angling, fly-fishing, netting, and spearfishing cater to various water bodies.

Understanding Fish Behavior

Understanding fish behavior and habitats is critical for fishing success. Insights into identifying feeding patterns, locating fish schools, and choosing the right bait enhance fishing efficiency.

DIY Fishing Gear and Equipment

Learn to craft improvised fishing gear from natural materials. From making fishing lines and hooks to constructing fish traps, readers gain skills for creating effective fishing tools.

Ice Fishing and Winter Techniques

Explore specialized fishing techniques for cold environments and frozen lakes. Insights into ice fishing equipment, hole drilling, and winter-specific baiting methods aid in successful fishing during icy conditions.

Deep-Sea and Offshore Fishing
Expand on fishing techniques suitable for deep-sea and offshore environments. Understanding deep-water species, tackle selection, and navigation enhances fishing experiences in open waters.
Aquatic Plant Identification for Fishing
Introduce the importance of understanding aquatic plants and their relevance to fishing. Knowledge of underwater vegetation aids in identifying potential fishing hotspots and selecting suitable bait for different species.

Effective Trapping Methods for Sustenance

Trapping Principles and Ethics
Understand the principles of trapping and ethical considerations. Detailed discussions on humane trapping, selective trapping, and trap placement minimize unnecessary harm to wildlife.

Types of Traps and Snares

Explore various types of traps and snares suitable for different games. From deadfalls and cage traps to snares and pit traps, readers gain insights into constructing and setting up effective trapping systems.

Baiting and Luring Techniques

Mastering baiting and luring strategies enhances trapping success. Insights into using natural baits, scents, and attractants lure game animals into traps or snares.

Natural Shelter and Trap Integration

Explore integrating traps with natural shelters or structures. Understanding how to camouflage traps within the environment increases their effectiveness while maintaining the overall concealment of the campsite.

Advanced Trap Modifications and Customizations

Discuss advanced modifications to conventional traps for specific game species. Tailoring traps based on animal behavior and preferences improves trapping efficiency and minimizes unintended catches.

Ethical Harvesting and Sustainability

Delve deeper into ethical considerations regarding trapping practices. Emphasize the importance of sustainable harvesting, trap maintenance, and minimizing environmental impact while relying on trapping for sustenance.

Expanding on these aspects provides a comprehensive guide, ensuring a deeper understanding of hunting, fishing, and trapping techniques across diverse environments and scenarios in wilderness or survival situations.

The Significance of Hunting, Fishing, and Trapping Skills

Chapter 7 underscores the importance of hunting, fishing, and trapping as essential survival skills. By mastering these techniques, individuals acquire the means to procure sustenance in diverse environments. The knowledge of prey behavior, fishing strategies, and trapping methods not only ensures a food source but also fosters a deeper connection with nature and self-reliance in challenging circumstances.

Chapter 8:Food Preservation and Food Storage

This is centered around the vital skill of food preservation and storage in the absence of modern conveniences. This includes techniques for preserving food without refrigeration, utilizing root cellars and natural storage methods, and employing drying, smoking, and canning techniques to ensure long-term food availability in off-grid living or survival scenarios.

Preserving Food Without Modern Conveniences

Understanding Food Spoilage and Preservation
Explore the science behind food spoilage and the principles of food preservation. Understanding the factors that cause food to spoil aids in

selecting appropriate preservation methods.

Traditional Preservation Techniques
Delve into historical preservation methods passed down through generations. Techniques such as fermentation, pickling, and using natural preservatives like salt or vinegar are explored for preserving a variety of food items.

Utilizing Natural Environmental Conditions
Understanding how environmental factors like temperature, humidity, and airflow affect food preservation. Readers learn to leverage natural conditions to store certain foods without the need for artificial refrigeration.

Indigenous Preservation Methods
Explore preservation techniques used by indigenous cultures worldwide. Insights into practices such as burying food in pits, fermenting with local ingredients, or utilizing natural oils

shed light on diverse preservation methodologies.

Herbal Preservation and Seasoning
Learn about the use of herbs and spices for food preservation and flavor enhancement. Discover herbs with natural preservative properties and how to incorporate them into food storage.

Food Waste Reduction and Preservation
Discuss strategies for reducing food waste through preservation. Techniques for utilizing leftovers, preserving excess produce, and repurposing scraps minimize wastage and maximize resource utilization.

Root Cellars and Natural Storage Methods

Building and Utilizing Root Cellars Detailed guidance on constructing root cellars for long-term food storage. Insights into cellar design, ventilation, and humidity control facilitate the creation of optimal storage conditions for various products.

Outdoor Cold Storage Techniques

Explore outdoor storage methods that utilize natural cold climates. Techniques like burying food caches in snow or using natural ice caves are discussed for preserving perishables in cold environments.

Utilizing Natural Materials for Storage

Learn about utilizing natural materials like sand, ash, or straw for preserving and insulating food items. Techniques for layering and packing food with natural materials aid in maintaining their quality over time.

Underground Storage Beyond Root Cellars

Explore other forms of underground storage, such as earth pits or caches. Understanding various underground storage methods aids in adapting to different environments and soil types.

Modern Adaptations and DIY Storage Solutions

Discuss modern adaptations of root cellars using readily available materials. Insights into building mini root cellars or converting existing structures for food storage cater to varying living situations.

Temperature and Humidity Regulation

Delve deeper into the principles of temperature and humidity control in storage. Techniques for managing airflow, insulation, and humidity levels within storage spaces are discussed for optimal food preservation.

Drying, Smoking, and Canning Techniques

Dehydration and Air-Drying Methods

Detailed instructions on air-drying and dehydrating food items. From sun-drying fruits to using dehydration racks for meats and vegetables, readers gain insights into preserving food through moisture removal.

Smoking and Curing for Preservation

Explore smoking and curing techniques for preserving meat and fish. From cold smoking to salt curing, readers learn about methods that not only preserve but also impart flavors to food.

Canning and Preserving in Jars

Comprehensive guidance on canning food in jars for long-term storage. Understanding canning equipment, sterilization, and proper sealing techniques ensures safe and effective preservation of various food items.

Solar Dehydration and Innovative Drying Methods

Explore innovative drying methods that utilize solar power. Insights into solar dehydrators or improvised drying racks enable food preservation in regions with abundant sunlight.

Advanced Smoking and Curing Techniques

Delve into advanced smoking and curing methods for a variety of meats and fish. Understanding cold smoking, hot smoking, or dry curing processes enhances preservation skills and culinary versatility.

Specialty Canning and Preservation Recipes

Introduce specialized canning recipes for preserving unique or seasonal produce. From jams and preserves to pickled delicacies, readers gain hands-on recipes for diverse preservation methods.

Empowerment Through Food Preservation

Chapter 8 serves as a guide to empower individuals with the knowledge and skills necessary for effective food preservation. By delving into indigenous methods, innovative adaptations, and specialized recipes, individuals not only ensure food security but also cultivate a deeper connection with food and a sustainable lifestyle in off-grid or self-reliant living situations.

Chapter 9: Off-Grid Cooking and Recipes

This focuses on off-grid cooking techniques and recipes, covering the art of creating meals with limited resources, exploring diverse cooking methods and tools, and providing a range of off-grid recipes for sustainable and nourishing meals in remote or self-reliant living situations.

Creating Meals with Limited Resources

Understanding Ingredient Substitution
Explore the art of ingredient substitution and improvisation in cooking. Readers learn how to adapt recipes by substituting ingredients with available alternatives, ensuring flexibility and creativity in cooking.

Seasonal Cooking and Harvest-Based Meals
Discuss the importance of seasonal cooking and utilizing harvested

produce. Insights into creating meals based on seasonal availability ensure freshness, variety, and sustainability in off-grid cooking.

One-Pot and Minimal Utensil Recipes
Delve into recipes that require minimal utensils and cookware. Discover the versatility of one-pot meals or recipes that utilize improvised cooking vessels, reducing the need for extensive kitchen equipment.

Cooking Methods and Tools

Open-Fire Cooking Techniques
Explore the art of cooking over open fires. Techniques for building and managing fires for cooking, such as grilling, roasting, or using Dutch ovens, offer insights into harnessing fire for culinary purposes.

Campfire Cooking Implements
Discuss essential campfire cooking tools and their uses. From tripods and grates to improvised skewers and pot

suspension systems, readers learn about tools for efficient cooking in outdoor settings.

Alternative Energy Cooking

Introduce alternative energy sources for cooking, such as solar ovens or rocket stoves. Understanding these methods broadens options for off-grid cooking, especially in areas with limited access to firewood or fuel.

Off-Grid Recipes for Sustainable Nutrition

Foraged and Wild Ingredients in Recipes

Explore recipes that incorporate foraged or wild ingredients. From wild greens in salads to foraged fruits in desserts, readers discover innovative ways to include nature's bounty in meals.

Preservation-Inspired Dishes

Explore recipes utilizing preserved foods, such as pickles, dried fruits, or cured meats. These recipes showcase how preserved ingredients can be transformed into flavorful and nutritious meals.

Plant-Based and Protein-Rich Recipes

Discuss recipes emphasizing plant-based ingredients or sustainable protein sources. From lentil stews to grilled vegetables or foraged mushroom dishes, these recipes prioritize nutrition and sustainability.

Culinary Resourcefulness in Off-Grid Living

Chapter 9 highlights the resourcefulness and creativity required for off-grid cooking. By providing techniques, tools, and a diverse range of recipes, individuals can nourish themselves sustainably and deliciously while embracing the challenges and rewards of cooking in remote or self-reliant living environments.

Chapter 10: Energy Independence

This is centered around achieving energy independence, focusing on harnessing solar and wind power, generating off-grid electricity, and managing sustainable energy sources for self-reliance in remote or off-grid living scenarios.

Harnessing Solar and Wind Power

Solar Energy Basics
Explore the fundamentals of solar energy capture. Readers learn about photovoltaic cells, solar panels, and the principles of converting sunlight into electricity. Insights into solar radiation and panel orientation aid in maximizing solar power generation.

Wind Energy Harvesting

Delve into harnessing wind power for off-grid electricity. Understanding wind turbine designs, wind patterns, and selecting suitable locations for wind power generation enhances knowledge about utilizing this renewable energy source.

Hybrid Systems and Energy Storage

Discuss hybrid systems that combine solar and wind energy. Insights into storing excess energy in batteries or using hybrid systems for continuous power supply cater to varying weather conditions and energy demands.

Generating Off-Grid Electricity

DIY Solar Panel Installation Comprehensive guidance on DIY solar panel installation. Step-by-step instructions and safety considerations empower individuals to set up their solar power systems, reducing reliance on external electricity sources.

Small-Scale Wind Turbines

Explore the installation and maintenance of small-scale wind turbines. Insights into selecting turbine size, tower placement, and safety measures aid in generating electricity from wind power in smaller setups.

Micro-Hydro Systems

Introduce micro-hydro systems for off-grid electricity generation. Understanding how to harness the energy from flowing water sources, such as streams or small rivers, provides another sustainable energy option.

Sustainable Energy Management

Energy Efficiency Strategies
Discuss energy-saving practices and efficiency measures for off-grid living. Tips on insulation, appliance selection,

and behavioral changes aid in optimizing energy use and minimizing wastage.

Grid-Tie and Off-Grid Systems Comparison

Explore the differences between grid-tie and off-grid systems. Understanding the pros and cons of each system helps individuals make informed decisions based on their energy needs and location.

Energy Monitoring and Maintenance

Discuss the importance of monitoring energy production and consumption. Insights into maintaining solar panels, wind turbines, and energy storage systems ensure optimal performance and longevity.

Empowerment Through Energy Independence

Chapter 10 underscores the significance of achieving energy independence in off-grid or remote living. By harnessing solar and wind power, generating off-grid electricity, and managing sustainable energy sources, individuals not only ensure a continuous and reliable power supply but also reduce their environmental impact while fostering self-reliance and sustainability.

Chapter 11: Building and Maintenance

This focuses on the construction of durable off-grid structures, maintenance of tools and equipment, and the principles of repairing and reusing resources in self-reliant living situations.

Constructing Durable Off-Grid Structures

Building Resilient Shelters

Discuss the fundamentals of constructing robust shelters in off-grid settings. Insights into selecting durable materials, framing techniques, and weather-resistant designs enhance the longevity of shelters.

Sustainable Building Materials

Explore eco-friendly and sustainable building materials suitable for off-grid structures. From recycled materials to locally sourced options, readers discover alternatives that minimize environmental impact.

Passive Design and Energy Efficiency
Delve into passive design principles for energy-efficient structures. Understanding aspects like orientation, insulation, and natural ventilation aids in creating comfortable and efficient living spaces.

Maintaining Tools and Equipment

Tool Maintenance and Sharpening
Discuss the importance of tool maintenance for longevity and efficiency. Insights into cleaning, sharpening, and preserving tools ensure their optimal performance in various off-grid tasks.

Improvisation and Tool Repair
Explore techniques for improvising tools and repairing equipment.

Understanding how to adapt tools for different tasks and troubleshoot common issues fosters resourcefulness and self-sufficiency.

Sustainable Tool Storage and Care
Discuss sustainable practices for tool storage and care. Insights into protecting tools from environmental elements and preventing corrosion or deterioration ensure their extended lifespan.

Repairing and Reusing Resources

Resourceful Repairs and Upcycling
Delve into resourceful repair techniques for salvaging and reusing materials. Insights into upcycling and repurposing resources minimize waste while providing innovative solutions.

Salvaging and Reclaiming Materials
Explore methods for salvaging materials from existing structures or discarded items. Understanding how to

reclaim and repurpose materials fosters a sustainable approach to construction and maintenance.

Waste Reduction and Circular Economy Discuss principles of waste reduction and circular economy concepts in construction. Exploring strategies to reduce waste and recycle materials aligns with eco-friendly off-grid living principles.

Self-Reliance Through Construction and Maintenance

Chapter 11 highlights the importance of construction durability, tool maintenance, and resourcefulness in off-grid living. By focusing on building robust structures, maintaining tools and equipment, and adopting a repair-and-reuse mentality, individuals cultivate self-reliance, sustainability, and resilience in their off-grid lifestyles.

Chapter 12: Community Building and Resilience

This centers around community building and resilience in off-grid living, focusing on establishing off-grid communities, fostering interactions with neighbors, sharing resources, and strengthening resilience through community bonds.

Establishing Off-Grid Communities

Collaborative Living Arrangements
Discuss the formation of off-grid communities based on shared values and sustainability principles. Insights into cooperative living, communal spaces, and collective decision-making enhance the foundation of off-grid communities.

Creating Shared Infrastructures

Explore the creation of shared infrastructures within off-grid communities. Collaborative efforts in building common facilities like water systems, renewable energy grids, or community gardens promote self-sufficiency.

Legal and Governance Frameworks

Discuss legal and governance considerations for off-grid communities. Insights into establishing community rules, agreements, and conflict resolution mechanisms foster harmonious living arrangements.

Interacting with Neighbors and Sharing Resources

Collaborative Resource Sharing

Explore the benefits of resource-sharing among off-grid neighbors. Discussing tools, surplus produce, or skills encourages mutual support and reduces individual reliance on external resources.

Bartering and Skill Exchange

Discuss the practice of bartering goods and skills within off-grid communities. Encouraging exchanges, such as trading surplus crops or sharing expertise, fosters a diverse and self-reliant community.

Community Events and Gatherings

Highlight the significance of community events in off-grid living. Organizing gatherings, workshops, or skill-sharing sessions strengthens social bonds and enhances the resilience of the community.

Strengthening Resilience Through Community Bonds

Mutual Support Networks

Explore the establishment of support networks within off-grid communities. Creating systems for mutual aid during emergencies or sharing knowledge enhances collective resilience.

Emotional and Mental Well-being

Discuss the role of community in supporting emotional and mental health. Promoting social connections, shared activities, and peer support contributes to overall well-being.

Emergency Preparedness and Response

Discussing community-wide emergency plans and responses. Understanding how to collectively prepare for and handle emergencies enhances the community's resilience and safety.

Building Resilient Off-Grid Communities

Chapter 12 emphasizes the importance of community building and resilience in off-grid living. By establishing supportive communities, fostering resource-sharing, and strengthening bonds among neighbors, individuals create resilient environments that thrive on collective efforts, mutual support, and shared values.

Conclusion

As we close the chapters on this comprehensive guide to off-grid living and self-reliance, it's crucial to reflect on the wealth of knowledge accumulated—skills honed, mindsets shifted, and the profound transformation toward a self-sufficient lifestyle.

Recap of Essential Survival Skills

Throughout this guide, we've explored a plethora of skills crucial for thriving in off-grid living scenarios. From mastering shelter building techniques to foraging for sustenance, acquiring fire-starting prowess to preserving food without modern conveniences—each skill forms a crucial piece in the mosaic of self-reliance.

Understanding how to source clean water, hunt and fish for sustenance, and harness renewable energy sources have empowered us to not just survive but flourish in environments disconnected from conventional amenities.

Embracing a Self-Reliant Lifestyle

Beyond the practical skills, this journey has been about embracing a mindset—a paradigm shift toward self-reliance and sustainability. It's about understanding our interconnectedness with nature, acknowledging the finite resources available, and conscientiously utilizing them.

The self-reliant lifestyle isn't just about survival; it's a celebration of resourcefulness, innovation, and harmony with the environment. It's about respecting the land, learning from its rhythms, and integrating these lessons into our daily lives.

Continuing the Path of Off-Grid Mastery

Our exploration into off-grid living has merely scratched the surface of a boundless journey toward mastery.

This concluding chapter isn't an endpoint but rather a threshold to continuous growth and refinement.

The path to off-grid mastery involves perpetual learning, adaptation, and innovation. It's about integrating new discoveries, refining existing skills, and embracing evolving technologies while staying grounded in the principles of sustainability and resilience.

Each step taken in this journey, each skill acquired, represents a building block in a life characterized by independence, stewardship of resources, and a deep connection with the natural world.

Final Thoughts

As we conclude this guide, remember that the journey toward self-reliance isn't a solitary one. It's a collective endeavor—a tapestry woven from the threads of shared knowledge, communal support, and interconnected lives.

Embrace the challenges, celebrate the triumphs, and continue fostering a community of like-minded individuals on this journey toward a more sustainable, self-reliant future. The path ahead might be unknown, but armed with the skills and the spirit of self-reliance, it's a journey worth undertaking.

So, here's to the pursuit of off-grid mastery—a journey not just of survival but of thriving, not merely of existing but of truly living in harmony with the world around us.

The adventure continues—let's tread this path of self-reliance together.

Printed in the USA
CPSIA information can be obtained
at www.ICGtesting.com
CBHW082201150924
14547CB00017B/2231